Bill,

May God bless yo

at Corban!

Ron Haas

2 Cor. 8:7

Simply Share

Bold, Grace-Based Giving

RON HAAS

the**TIMOTHY**group
STEWARDSHIP RESOURCES

Simply Share — Bold, Grace-Based Giving
Copyright © 2015 Ron Haas

All rights reserved. No part of this publication may be reproduced without the prior permission of the author.

All scripture quotations, unless otherwise indicated, are taken from the Holy Bible, New International Version®, NIV®. Copyright ©1973, 1978, 1984, 2011 by Biblica, Inc.™ Used by permission of Zondervan. All rights reserved worldwide. www.zondervan.com. The "NIV" and "New International Version" are trademarks registered in the United States Patent and Trademark Office by Biblica, Inc.™

Scripture quotations marked (MSG) are taken from *The Message.* Copyright © 1993, 1994, 1995, 1996, 2000, 2001, 2002. Used by permission of NavPress Publishing Group.

For information on how to purchase multiple copies of *Simply Share* for your small group, Sunday school class or congregation, please contact:

The Timothy Group
1663 Sutherland Dr. SE
Grand Rapids, MI 49508
616-224-4060
www.timothygroup.com
simplyshare@timothygroup.com

Cover Design: Sarah P. Merrill
Interior Design: Michelle VanGeest

ISBN 0-9788585-4-9
Printed in the United States of America.

Simply Share

Bold, Grace-Based Giving

CONTENTS

Introduction 7

1   Give Beyond Your Ability / 2 Cor. 8:1–5 11
    Ally Shank—Sharing a Determined Gift

2   Excel in the Grace of Giving / 2 Cor. 8:6–7 21
    Jake Canniff—Sharing a Growing Gift

3   Become Poor / 2 Cor. 8:9 29
    Nam Kim—Sharing a Refreshing Gift

4   Prove Your Love / 2 Cor. 8:8, 24; 9:3–5, 13 37
    Sue and Scott Gardner—Sharing an Obedient Gift

5   Sow Generously / 2 Cor. 9:6–10 45
    Gene and Elaine Getz—Sharing a Joyful Gift

6   Be Generous on Every Occasion / 2 Cor. 9:11–15 53
    Paul Johnson—Sharing a Living Gift

Conclusion / Generous and Willing to Share 61
    Charlie DeLano—Sharing a Sacrificial Gift

Final Thoughts from the Author 65

Addendum:
    2 Corinthians 8–9 (NIV) 69
    Principles to Simply Share 73
    Scripture Index 75
    Notes 77
    About the Author 79

INTRODUCTION

Sharing is not easy. Bill and Melinda Gates and Warren Buffett formed The Giving Pledge to challenge the world's billionaires to give half of their wealth through philanthropy either during their lifetime or in their will.[1] So far 115 billionaires have signed up, but Buffett has discovered that not everyone is eager to part with their hard-earned money. "I've gotten a lot of yeses when I've called people. But I've gotten a lot of noes too. And I am tempted, because I've been calling people with a billion dollars or more, I've been tempted to think that if they can't sign up for 50 percent, maybe I should write a book on how to get by on $500 million. Because apparently there's a lot of people that don't really know how to do it."[2]

If people who have so much money have a hard time letting go, how can those of us who don't have as much learn to share? The simple truth is we are wired for selfishness. Parents can testify that one of the first words a child speaks is, "Mine!" Dr. William Sears, pediatrician and father of eight children, notes, "True sharing implies empathy, the ability to get into another's mind and see things from their viewpoint. Children are seldom capable of true empathy under the age of six."[3] Unfortunately, some of us never seem to develop true empathy.

In 2 Corinthians 8–9, Paul introduces us to some ordinary Christians who displayed an extraordinary willingness to share.

The church in Jerusalem was suffering under persecution and famine, so Paul organized a relief effort and asked all the churches in Asia to share with their brothers and sisters. The believers in Corinth were quick to give and promised more. Paul told of the Corinthians' generosity everywhere he went. The Macedonian churches were so motivated by the Corinthians' gift that they surprised Paul with a generous gift of their own. Meanwhile, back in Corinth, the church was slow to follow through with their promised gift, so Paul penned 2 Corinthians in part to spur them into action.

The history of Macedonia provides an interesting backdrop to 2 Corinthians. In its glory years, Macedonia was an economic powerhouse. Alexander the Great (356–323 BC) became ruler at age 20 and quickly extended his empire to Europe, Egypt, and India. As Alexander marched through Babylon and Persia he raided their royal treasuries of more than 7,290 tons of gold and silver. The loot was so massive that Alexander had to round up more than 20,000 pack mules and 5,000 camels to carry his spoils back home.[4] Alexander cultivated the arts as no patron had done before him. Skilled artisans created gold-overlaid furniture, expensive dresses embroidered with purple and gold, and precious objects of every kind. It's estimated that the royal mint in Amphipolis struck more than 13 million gold coins with Alexander's image. The Macedonians were the billionaires of their day and they spent their money on themselves.

However, Macedonia's superpower status didn't last long. Alexander's death at the age of 33 threw the world into chaos as his generals broke up his empire into little pieces for themselves. Eventually, Rome corralled Macedonia back into its original borders, imposed high taxes, and left a few legions around to deal with any late payments. Rome's severe tribute on Macedonia produced such a financial windfall that the Senate exempted citizens living in Rome from personal income taxes for 120 years.[5]

The city of Corinth and the cities of Macedonia provide a stark contrast. At one point the Macedonians were extremely wealthy, but at this moment in history they were extremely poor. Corinth, on the other hand, was a major urban center and probably the wealthiest city in Greece.[6] The contrast between the churches of Macedonia and the church in Corinth is just as

The Macedonian church was poor, but willing to share; the Corinthians were rich, but reluctant to share.

vivid. The Macedonian church was poor, but willing to share; the Corinthians were rich, but reluctant to share.

This reluctance to share still limits the church's impact today. The Barna Group reports that in 2012, only 12% of born again Christians (both evangelicals and non-evangelicals) gave 10% or more of their annual income to a church or non-profit organization. This percentage hasn't changed for the past decade.[7] Whether they have a little or a lot, Christians are called to share. The writer to the Hebrews reminds us, "And do not forget to do good and to share with others, for with such sacrifices God is pleased" (Heb. 13:16). In 2 Corinthians 8–9, Paul teaches six key principles about sharing:

1. **Give Beyond Your Ability** (2 Cor. 8:1–5)
2. **Excel in the Grace of Giving** (2 Cor. 8:6–7)
3. **Become Poor** (2 Cor. 8:9)
4. **Prove Your Love** (2 Cor. 8:8, 24; 9:3–5, 13)
5. **Sow Generously** (2 Cor. 9:6–10)
6. **Be Generous on Every Occasion** (2 Cor. 9:11–15)

Sharing is for Christians of every age group—children through senior citizens. To illustrate this truth, each lesson in this study includes a testimony from someone who is learning to share. Group discussion questions are also suggested after each lesson to help you apply these principles.

Billionaires aren't the only ones who struggle with sharing. We all need to loosen our grip on our possessions and learn to simply share.

1

GIVE BEYOND YOUR ABILITY

*"And now, brothers and sisters, we want you to know about the grace that God has given the Macedonian churches. In the midst of a very severe trial, their overflowing joy and their extreme poverty welled up in rich generosity. For I testify that they gave as much as they were able, **and even beyond their ability.** Entirely on their own, they urgently pleaded with us for the privilege of sharing in this service to the Lord's people. And they exceeded our expectations: They gave themselves first of all to the Lord, and then by the will of God also to us." (2 Cor. 8:1–5)*

There is nothing more powerful than seeing the grace of God reflected in a person's life. It's thrilling to hear how someone came to faith in Christ, overcame an addiction, restored a broken relationship, or was miraculously healed from a physical affliction. These stories of God's grace never get old. Each one challenges us to trust God even more in our own walk with him.

Sometimes the grace of God shows up in someone's life in such a powerful way that it takes us by surprise. In 2 Corinthians 8–9, Paul shares the inspiring testimony of the Macedonian believers, whose faith was revealed through their extreme generosity. Paul was collecting money for the believers in Jerusalem who were suffering from persecution and poverty. The Macedonian believers' incredible response despite their own poverty teaches us how to give beyond our ability.

Sharing originates with God.

What does God's grace mean to you? Jesus Christ came into the world to pay the penalty for our sin and provide salvation. If you have repented from your sin and received the gift of eternal life, you have experienced God's grace firsthand. Saving grace is just the beginning. Paul wrote that God's plan is that "in the coming ages he might show the incomparable riches of his grace, expressed in his kindness to us in Christ Jesus" (Eph. 2:7). God's grace is amazing and limitless. He offers salvation by grace and he also offers believers abundant grace to live a new life. John writes "We have all received grace in place of grace already given" (John 1:16). There is a never-ending supply of God's grace in our lives. He gives us all that we need and then he gives more. This is an incredible truth when you think about grace in relation to your capacity to share with others.

> **In the midst of a very severe trial, their overflowing joy and their extreme poverty welled up in rich generosity.** (2 Cor. 8:2)

Grace means "gift." Paul's use of the word *grace* in 2 Corinthians 8–9 six times in this passage emphasizes that we have the ability to share only because God has poured out his blessing on us. The Macedonians didn't give to earn favor with God or gain recognition from others. Their sharing wasn't motivated by the hope that God would repay them bountifully. They gave generously simply because they were recipients of God's generous gift of grace. Paul expresses it best later in his letter when he says, "Thanks be to God for his indescribable gift!" (2 Cor. 9:15).

Sharing is not limited by our resources.

The Macedonians were not wealthy. Paul describes their situation as a "very severe trial" and "extreme poverty" (2 Cor. 8:2). Sometimes we deceive ourselves into thinking that we don't have enough money to give, or that sharing only applies to "rich" Christians. Paul shared that the Macedonians "gave as much as they were able, and even beyond their ability" (2 Cor. 8:3). From Paul's perspective, they gave with abandon because their "overflowing joy" propelled them to "rich generosity."

How does someone "give beyond their ability"? In 1 Kings 17:7–16, God sent Elijah to a poor widow in the village of Zarephath. When the prophet arrived at the village well, he asked her for a drink of water and a piece of bread. Sharing a drink of water with Elijah was easy; it only took a little time and effort, but giving him bread seemed impossible because it would cost her everything she had. Elijah's request forced this widow to look at her resources, as meager as they were, and trust God's promise that he would meet her needs. By faith, she made a loaf of bread for Elijah and God honored her obedience. That handful of flour and little jar of oil sustained her, her son, and Elijah for the rest of the famine. Her faith enabled her to give "beyond her ability."

When you look at your bank balance, do you wrestle with the question, "If I give, will I have enough to meet my needs?" Giving beyond your ability requires you to exercise faith with your limited resources and trust God to add "grace upon grace." It's attempting great things for God and trusting him for the results.

Sharing is a privilege.

Paul was so surprised by the Macedonians' generosity that he was reluctant to take their gift. However, "they urgently pleaded with us for the privilege of sharing in this service to the Lord's people" (2 Cor. 8:4). What a remarkable scene! Paul didn't think they could "afford" to give. He focused on the Macedonians' extreme poverty, but they were determined to serve the Lord and insisted on getting in on the action. They demonstrated the same sense of urgency as the man who discovered a treasure hidden in a field (see Matt. 13:44). He immediately sold all he had and purchased the field. He acted with boldness because he recognized the value. The Macedonians gave with boldness because they recognized the blessings of sharing. To them, giving was a privilege, and they refused to take "no" for an answer.

Instead of approaching sharing as a duty or drudgery, we should view our gifts as an opportunity to partner with what God is doing in the lives of others. Henry Blackaby reminds us, "When you give...you send ripples out through the whole kingdom of God. You contribute to the process by which people see the faithfulness of God and come to trust in Him...You are a co-worker with God in a much bigger picture than you can see."[8] The Macedonians understood the eternal value of their gift.

Share your heart first.

The key that unlocked the Macedonians' generosity is that they gave their hearts first to the Lord, and then gave to the cause. Sharing is the natural response for believers who are completely sold out to God's will. When God has your heart, it just makes sense to honor him with your possessions. How we handle money reveals the true condition of our hearts. "For where your treasure is, there your heart will be also" (Matt. 6:21). What does your bank statement say about your heart? Money has a way of clouding our perspective about what's really important in life. We are tempted to chase money and things and miss out on "the life that is truly life" (see 1 Tim. 6:19). In the parable of the four types of soil, Jesus warned that riches can prevent someone from responding to the

Gospel: "The worries of this life, the deceitfulness of wealth and the desires for other things come in and choke the word, making it unfruitful" (Mark 4:18–19).

The testimony of the Macedonian believers should inspire us to think differently about our giving priorities. They didn't give because of Paul's tear-jerking story, but because they wanted to serve God by sharing. They could have used their dire circumstances as an excuse for not giving. Even Paul wouldn't have condemned them for focusing on the needs of their families instead of giving to others. But because they had dedicated themselves to serving the Lord, they saw sharing as an expression of the grace of God in their lives. We have received that same grace, and we should respond in the very same way.

> "When you give...you are a co-worker with God in a much bigger picture than you can see." — Henry Blackaby

God's grace gives us the faith to give beyond our ability.

Ally Shank—Sharing a Determined Gift

Katie Davis is changing the world one child at a time. As an eighteen-year-old senior class president and homecoming queen she had everything the world said was important. She "dated cute boys, wore cute shoes, and drove a cute sports car."[9] In December of 2006, Katie took a short mission trip to Uganda that turned her life inside out. She went back the following summer, intending to teach kindergarten at an orphanage for one year and then return home to a normal life, but God had other plans.

The extreme poverty Katie experienced in Uganda shocked her. Impoverished families have little hope for their children. There are few government-run schools and tuition for privately operated schools is beyond the reach of most families. God laid it on Katie's heart to start a child sponsorship program to help orphaned or vulnerable children go to school.

Originally Katie's goal was to reach 40 children in the sponsorship program, but in less than a year she was helping 150 children. In 2008, Katie formed Amazima Ministries International, which currently sponsors more than 600 children. A $300 gift provides one child with an education for one year, school supplies, three hot meals each day, spiritual discipleship, and medical care. Now the mother of 13 adopted daughters, Katie reflects, "I never planned this for my life. It was just one little step of obedience at a time."

Eight-year-old Ally Shank began reading *Kisses for Katie* with her family and decided to raise $300 to sponsor a child. She opened a lemonade stand at her grandma's house with a yellow poster board that said, "All sales go to support a Ugandan child." Ally stood in the sun for several hours and made a total of three dollars. Undeterred, she tucked that three dollars away in a special jar and was determined to see it eventually become $300.

Later that summer, Ally organized a garage sale. For two days she stood by a table full of trinkets and toys with her sign, "All sales go to support a Ugandan child." It rained all day the first day, but the second day her friends came to support her and brought some things to sell as well. Ally made about $20 and was elated, but she was still determined to earn $300.

Her next idea was to braid and sell bracelets. Throughout the school year, Ally told anyone who would listen she was selling bracelets to raise money to support a child in Uganda. Sunday school teachers, people at church, neighbors, friends, and family all began buying these simple thread bracelets for a donated price...usually between five and 20 dollars. Ally's money was adding up.

Ally spent a week with her grandparents, and her grandma offered to make muffins and other baked goods to sell at a local Christian college to support Ally's mission to help a child in Uganda. For three mornings, Ally and her grandma walked around campus asking students and faculty if they would like to donate to a good cause and get a sweet treat as well. Everyone loved seeing a little girl's heart shine brightly for others. Ally sold almost all the baked goods and earned the rest of the money.

Ally not only raised $300 for a child in Uganda, she exceeded her own expectations and raised a total of $500. She took a small step of obedience like Katie Davis and God helped her complete her goal. When Ally went online and clicked the Donate button, her face was glowing. Her very next words were, "I'm so excited that I already have half the money to support another child!" Because of Ally's heart for the children, her family saved enough money to support a second child.

(See Ally's letter to Katie on the next page!)

Dear Katie,
You are Super awesome! I look up and want to be like you when I grow up. I read your book and was inspired and saw God work in your life. So I started raising money. It started from a lemanand stand and 25¢ sip and ended up raising more than $300! I can't belive you sacerficed so, so, SO much! Even college! I am praying for you! I learned through you that if your big or small you can still acomplish big things!! :) I was 8 when I raised that money. Now I am 10. Me and my friend (Mary) are still working to raise more money. If you need anything just tell us. We will always be by your side!

Love
Ally Jo Shank

Kisses
From Katie

Discussion Questions

1. How should the grace of God impact our giving?

   _____

   _____

2. How were the Macedonian believers able to give generously even when they didn't have much to share?

   _____

   _____

3. How would you encourage a friend who believes he can't afford to share?

   _____

   _____

4. In what ways do you consider giving to be a privilege?

   _____

   _____

5. Share a personal lesson you have learned about generous giving. If you have children, how are you modeling sharing to them?

   _____

   _____

   _____

   _____

Personal Reflection

How does my willingness to share reflect God's grace in my life?

2
EXCEL IN THE GRACE OF GIVING

*"So we urged Titus, just as he had earlier made a beginning, to bring also to completion this act of grace on your part. But since you excel in everything—in faith, in speech, in knowledge, in complete earnestness and in the love we have kindled in you—**see that you also excel in this grace of giving.**"* (2 Cor. 8:6–7)

"Satisfactory underperformance" occurs when a business or an organization gets stuck in a rut and begins to simply accept things as they are without really pushing toward what could be possible. Christians can fall into the same type of satisfactory underperformance when they approach their faith in a half-hearted way and become complacent. Paul's challenge to generous giving is a call to break out of our comfort zones and trust God with our resources.

Sharing demonstrates spiritual maturity.

Paul praised the church in Corinth for excelling in five key areas: faith, speech, knowledge, complete earnestness, and love and

21

then he challenged them to give with the same enthusiasm. We encourage new believers to grow in these same ways: Walk by faith. Share the Gospel. Read and memorize the Bible. Be genuine. Love. We should be just as concerned that we develop the spiritual discipline of giving. How often have you heard a convicting sermon about generous giving and responded, "Great sermon, Pastor!" For Paul, extraordinary giving was just another mark of spiritual growth.

We will never reach a point in our Christian walk where we have arrived—when we trust God completely, always say the right thing, understand every-

Paul's challenge to generous giving is a call to break out of our comfort zones and trust God with our resources.

thing about God's Word, have the passion we should, or love others as we ought. There will always be areas in our Christian life that we can improve—that's especially true when it comes to generous giving.

When Zacchaeus trusted Christ as Savior, the impact on his life was dramatic and immediate: "Look, Lord! Here and now I give half of my possessions to the poor, and if I have cheated anybody out of anything, I will pay back four times the amount" (Luke 19:8). The grace of God instantly transformed Zacchaeus's heart from greed to generosity.

Sharing is best expressed in community.

Christians can't grow spiritually in a vacuum. Our faith is strengthened as we walk with others in community. We learn to speak the truth with grace as we interact with others. We grow in our knowledge as "iron sharpens iron" (Prov. 27:17). Our love for one another deepens as we put our faith into action. The same is true with giving. We learn how to be generous when we see it modeled in someone else. But it's more than that. Sharing strengthens the bond between believers because both the giver and the receiver benefit from the relationship. Those believers in Macedonia who gave generously felt a special kinship with the believers in Jerusalem who needed their help, and vice versa.

It wasn't that the Corinthian believers hadn't given anything. They were actually the first church to respond to Paul's relief appeal for the Jerusalem believers. In fact, it was the Corinthians' initial response that inspired the Macedonians to give. Paul reminded the Corinthians just how powerful their giving example had been: "Your enthusiasm has stirred most of them to action" (2 Cor. 9:2). It's ironic that now Paul uses the generosity of the Macedonians to prompt the Corinthians to finish what they started. That's how Christian community works. God uses our obedience to "spur one another on toward love and good deeds" (Heb. 10:24). Solomon understood the power of community when he wrote, "Two are better than one...If either of them falls down, one can help the other up" (Eccl. 4:9–10). The Corinthians needed the Macedonians' example of rich generosity to snap them out of their satisfactory underperformance.

Sharing demands excellence, not mediocrity.

Do you give more now than when you first came to faith? To "excel in the grace of giving" means that you strive to give as much as possible. Paul compares the pursuit of spiritual excellence to athletes preparing for a competition: "Everyone who competes in the games goes into strict training" (1 Cor. 9:25). Professional athletes push themselves with rigorous training workouts. It takes mental and physical discipline to reach the top of their game. Those who live by the motto "No pain—No gain" realize that you must endure some pain to reach your goal.

Christians who excel in giving can only do so because they have disciplined themselves to manage their finances well. Nathan

W. Morris teaches, "The speed of your success is limited only by your dedication and what you're willing to sacrifice."[10] This principle helps you achieve your financial goals and also helps you achieve your giving goals. By carefully managing your money, you will have more resources to be generous. Extraordinary giving doesn't just happen; it requires a plan and the discipline to follow through. Anyone can be an average giver, but to excel you have to make sacrifices. It costs something to be generous, but the short-term pain is worth the reward.

Sharing is motivated by grace, not law.

Many Christians view "tithing" as the giving standard based on the pattern established in the Old Testament. A closer look reveals that Moses actually outlined a three-tithe system for the children of Israel. Landowners were required to give 10 percent of their grain, new wine, olive oil, and the firstborn of their herds and flocks to support the Levites (see Lev. 27:30–34). A second 10 percent called the festival tithe was used so the family could travel to Jerusalem and worship (see Deut. 14:22–27). Every third year the Israelites were to give another 10 percent to help the fatherless, the foreigner, and the widow (see Deut. 26:12; 14:28–29).

Old Testament giving was an act of worship: "Three times a year all your men must appear before the LORD your God at the place he will choose: at the Festival of Unleavened Bread, the Festival of Weeks and the Festival of Tabernacles. No one should appear before the LORD empty-handed: Each of you

> **Extraordinary giving doesn't just happen; it requires a plan and the discipline to follow through.**

must bring a gift in proportion to the way the LORD your God has blessed you" (Deut. 16:16–17). They were required to attend and they were required to give. When you combine this threefold tithe,

the total required giving for an Old Testament believer amount-
ed to about 23 percent. On top of this, they paid a temple tax and
were encouraged to give freewill offerings.

As Christians, we are not bound by the Mosaic Law because
Christ fulfilled all of its requirements. Paul could have framed
generous giving in terms of a specific amount or percentage, but
instead he encouraged the Corinthians to "excel in the grace of giving." To excel means to "abound." John uses the word to describe
the twelve baskets of barley loves that remained "over and above"
after Jesus fed the five thousand (John 6:13 KJV). We should approach our giving with this "over and above" attitude.

Tithing can be a helpful practice to teach systematic giving.
Some Christians start with 10 percent and try to increase their
giving every year. They grow from giving a percentage to giving in
proportion to the way God has blessed them. Through God's grace
we are blessed with the boundless "riches of Christ" (Eph. 3:8).
Shouldn't we give back to him with the same abundance? Has your
giving become stale and mundane? What's holding you back from
excelling in the grace of giving?

Jake Canniff—Sharing a Growing Gift

If you ran into Jake Canniff while he was working part-time at a lo-cal produce market, you might think you are seeing a typical teenager. But Jake is not your average high school senior—he passionately loves the Lord, serves in his local church, volunteers at a food pantry, and is learning how to give. Here's Jake's story.

"God is teaching me so much about sharing. My parents and my grandparents modeled sharing for me with their attitude that money is a loan from God. As a child I didn't understand what it meant to sac-rifice. Now that I'm older, I realize that it's a big step of faith to give the first part of my money to the Lord. I have friends who give 10 percent or more, but I also have friends who would rather spend their money on stuff like new video games or car insurance. Mary's story in John 12 re-ally inspires me. When she poured out her bottle of expensive perfume on Jesus' head, Judas thought she was wasting her money, but she was willing to give her best—no matter what others thought. If God calls me to give a little of what I have to help expand the kingdom, it's really not that much to ask.

"I give every week and basically follow the 10 percent guideline. When I get overtime or some unexpected money, I give more. Giving 10 percent is a good thing, but I almost think of it as a minimum. As Chris-tians we are called to give. It doesn't matter how much money you have. When you have a limited amount it means more to you. It's a humbling thing to share. We receive good things from God, but we shouldn't just be receivers; we should be givers. I help out with a kids' food basket program that takes two hours once a month. Sharing builds your faith. When you give so others can hear and receive the Gospel, these new believers grow in their faith and start giving, so even more can hear. It's a constant cycle.

"God has met my needs in many surprising ways. I wanted to go on a mission trip with my church youth group this past summer. It cost $75 and I was $15 short. On the final sign-up day, I had $15 in my pocket—but it was my tithe money. I didn't feel right about spending it for my expenses, so I put it in God's hands, gave my tithe, and believed that he would provide. When I got home, I noticed a $20 bill blowing in the wind on my porch. It was pretty amazing.

"Sharing gives me lots of joy. I give to a small ministry called Victory in Christ. Kirk Kouchnerkavich is a college student who helps teens struggling with depression, suicide, and self-harm. He goes to hardcore metal shows and spreads the Gospel. On a recent band tour, six teens trusted Christ! Kirk shared a cool update about one guy with severe depression who accepted Christ after a concert. I love knowing that I helped Kirk plant this seed of faith. Maybe I wasn't there in person, but my gift was a part of it.

"To excel in the grace of giving means that you take a step beyond what you are sharing and strive for more. In school, you shouldn't just settle for a 'B,' but strive for an 'A.' Some people are satisfied with giving 10 percent, but why not strive for 15 or 20 percent or more? A lady once asked me why I give. I'm not forced to give; I give because I feel this drive. Christ gave the ultimate gift when he died on the cross. If he asks me to give up something so others can hear the Gospel—of course I'm going to do it."

Discussion Questions

1. Why do you think only 12 percent of born again Christians give 10 percent or more of their annual income to a church or non-profit organization?

   _____

   _____

2. What excuses do Christians use for not giving generously?

   _____

   _____

3. The Macedonians were motivated by the Corinthians' willingness to share. How has someone else's generosity encouraged you to share?

   _____

   _____

4. In what ways is sharing a spiritual discipline?

   _____

   _____

5. How has tithing influenced your giving?

   _____

   _____

Personal Reflection

What specific changes must I make to excel in the grace of giving?

3

BECOME POOR

*"For you know the grace of our Lord Jesus Christ, that though he was rich, **yet for your sake he became poor**, so that you through his poverty might become rich"* (2 Cor. 8: 9).

Financial expert Dave Ramsey makes a humorous comparison about listening to the wrong counselors: "Broke people giving financial advice is like a shop teacher with missing fingers."[11] It's probably not too smart to ask someone who doesn't have any money how to invest your money. But when it comes to generous giving, we can learn a lot from people of faith who don't have many resources. Jesus noticed the widow who gave her two copper coins and commented that she gave more than the rich people because they gave out of their wealth, "but she, out of her poverty, put in everything—all she had to live on" (Mark 12:44). The rich were tipping God, but she gave it all. Paul continues his lesson on generous giving by emphasizing Jesus' poverty.

Sharing puts true wealth in perspective.

We don't often think of Jesus as rich. Instead, we remember his humble birth, the fact that he had no place to lay his head, or that he was buried in a borrowed tomb. But before the manger, Jesus enjoyed the riches of heaven as he dwelled with the Father in perfect equality and unity. We can't begin to comprehend the riches of heaven. John gives us a glimpse of the streets of gold, the foundation laid with twelve different precious stones and each gate carved from a single pearl (see Rev. 21:10–21). When it comes to wealth, the Psalmist declares that God doesn't need our offerings because he owns "the cattle on a thousand hills" (Psalm 50:10). Jesus was rich beyond measure, but because he valued us more, he willingly laid aside all of his privileges.

Wealth is seductive. It lures us with the illusion of satisfaction and security, but provides neither. Jesus told a parable about a rich farmer who was so impressed with his bumper crop that he decided to tear down his barns and build bigger barns to hold his surplus. His goal was to amass so much stuff that he could kick back and take life easy. "But God said to him, 'You fool! This very night your life will be demanded from you. Then who will get what you have prepared for yourself?' This is how it will be with whoever stores up things for themselves but is not rich toward God" (Luke 12:20–21). His wealth blurred his vision of what really matters in life. This man poured all of his energy into earthly things, but forgot to invest in spiritual things.

> **Wealth is seductive. It lures us with the illusion of satisfaction and security, but provides neither.**

Sharing denies self.

Jesus said, "Whoever wants to be my disciple must deny themselves and take up their cross daily and follow me" (Luke 9:23). Following Christ starts with the decision to deny yourself. Christians who give generously can do so only because they have disciplined themselves to manage their finances well. Each of us has a limited amount of money. We must decide how we will save, invest, and give it. Reluctant givers have a hard time sharing because they get distracted with everything else they could do with the money. Generous giving means that we deny ourselves to benefit others. We can spend "our" money on our pleasures, or we can become disciples and invest God's money to advance the kingdom.

Wealth is dangerous because it promotes an attitude of self-reliance and pride. Why trust God for your daily bread when you can just go buy it? Money is not the root of all evil. The "love of money" is the root of all evil (1 Tim. 6:10). Paul warns that greed can derail our Christian walk. "Those who want to get rich fall into temptation and a trap and into many foolish and harmful desires that plunge people into ruin and destruction" (1 Tim. 6:9). It's not sinful to be ambitious. The Lord honors hard work (see Prov. 14:23). The problem comes when we begin to live for money instead of God. Sharing is the perfect antidote for selfishness.

Sharing is intentional.

Paul wrote that Jesus *became* poor. This was not a casual decision; it was a choice to be obedient to the Father's redemption plan. Jesus obeyed with the full understanding of the price he would pay. Because of his great love, he was willing to become poor for us.

It's easy just to drop a few dollars in the offering plate without thinking, but serious giving decisions can't be made on a whim. The cost is too high. Jesus planned to make a difference with his gift and it cost him everything. When David asked to purchase the threshing floor for the new temple, the owner pleaded with him to take the land as a gift. David responded, "No, I insist on paying the full price. I will not take for the LORD what is yours, or sacrifice a burnt offering that costs me nothing" (1 Chron. 21:24).

In Paul's first letter to them he instructed the Corinthians to approach giving in a systematic way. "On the first day of every week, each one of you should set aside a sum of money in keeping with your income, saving it up, so that when I come no collections will have to be made" (1 Cor. 16:2). Paul's giving plan is very practi-

Sharing is the perfect antidote for selfishness.

cal. It should be consistent, "every week." It should be personal, "each one of you." It should be proportionate, "in keeping with your income." And it should be intentional, "saving it up." Paul wanted the Corinthians to avoid casual, spur-of-the-moment giving.

Sharing produces eternal results.

Jesus gave up the riches of heaven so that we could become rich beyond measure—not monetarily, but spiritually. Paul describes this gift as "the incomparable riches of his grace" (Eph. 2:7), and "the boundless riches of Christ" (Eph. 3:8). He sacrificed his life for our eternal benefit. We follow Christ's example when we share so others can hear the message of grace. In a sense, our sacrifice to "become poor" by giving to our local church, missionaries, and parachurch ministries enables others to become "rich" with the good news of Jesus Christ.

You can lay up treasures on earth and watch them fade away, or you can lay up treasures in heaven where they will last for eternity. A person with an earthly mind-set values things more than people. Believers with an eternal perspective of wealth value people more than things. Moses understood the importance of becoming poor in this life in order to become rich in the next. "He regarded disgrace for the sake of Christ as of greater value than the treasures of Egypt, because he was looking ahead to his reward"

(Heb. 11:26). He could have been incredibly successful by the world's standard, but he gave it all up for something better.

The best investment you could ever make is to "Store up for yourselves treasures in heaven" (Matt. 6:20). Serious giving demands that you make a choice. Will you tear down your barns and build bigger ones to store more possessions, or will you be "rich toward God"? (Luke 12:21). One generous giver reflected, "I've made many investments that failed, but I've never regretted anything that I've given to the Lord."

Becoming poor is difficult because we are wired to accumulate possessions for our own enjoyment. Psalm 132:1 adds insight to King David's purchase of the land for the Temple, "Lord, remember David and all his self-denial." He could have spent his treasury of gold on himself, but David's priority was to find a dwelling place for the Lord—no matter the cost. We face the same question, "Will we spend what we have on ourselves, or will we release our grip on our resources to advance the Gospel?"

Nam Kim—Sharing a Refreshing Gift

God called me into ministry, so I moved from Seoul, South Korea, to attend seminary in Kentucky. Before I left for seminary, a friend encouraged me to invest money so that it would grow faster than in my savings account. For almost three years, I faithfully put $100 per month in a mutual fund. I was able to cover my expenses with the money I had saved and income from a part-time job. As an international student, I was only permitted to work just a few hours per week on campus. Unfortunately, at the end of my second year the global financial crisis hit and wiped out my savings. The exchange rate caused the South Korean won to decline and my tuition, room, and board doubled. Because there was only one year left, I went back home to work a summer job so I could continue seminary—but it wasn't enough. I blamed God for my troubles and prayed, "God, I am studying to serve you, why are you making it so difficult?"

A friend invited me to the fourth anniversary of the founding of a small Korean church in Seoul. A lady whom I had met that Sunday called me the following week and wanted to get together. When we met, she handed me an envelope that contained a check for $10,000. I cried tears of joy. It was enough to cover my last year of seminary. I thanked her and she responded, "The Spirit of God told me to give it to you. It is a gift freely given to you as Christ has freely given to me." I had studied theology, but this woman's faith and mercy taught me more about following Christ than any lecture I've ever heard.

I flew back to seminary for my last year. That fall I learned about one student from Africa who was struggling financially and one church member who needed help for his short-term mission trip to Cambodia. The Spirit of God said to me, "Why don't you share with them what you have received?" I argued with God, "I'm a poor, struggling student. I need the money. Why do I have to share with others?" But God kept speaking to me. I divided $1,000 between two envelopes and gave it to my friends to share anonymously with the needy student and church member for his mission trip. I heard that when they opened the envelope they praised God, just as I had praised God for meeting my needs.

A few weeks later, one of my close Christian brothers from Korea called me and said, "Our small group at church has been collecting money for six months to donate to someone who is struggling. We decided to give it to you and we are sending you $1,000." Then God surprised me with another gift. An unknown donor put $1,000 in my bank account with the note, "We love you."

Before this experience, I had fears about money, but a kind woman's generosity proved to me that God would care for me. He is faithful. Now I know what it means to be a cheerful giver. It was hard to sacrifice a portion of my money. I tried to rationalize all the reasons why I couldn't share, but eventually I acted on the voice of God and he blessed my obedience. I used to be hesitant about receiving a gift from someone, but now I'm happy to receive because I try to share a portion of that gift with someone else.

God is training me that money belongs to him. It's better to share it than keep it. I've experienced Proverbs 11:25: "A generous person will prosper; whoever refreshes others will be refreshed." Saving money saves self, but sharing money saves souls.

Discussion Questions

1. How is the rich farmer's attitude toward wealth similar to attitudes of people today? (Luke 12:16–21)

   _____

   _____

2. What are some of the temptations or traps for people who want to get rich? (1 Tim. 6:9)

   _____

   _____

3. What lessons can we learn from David's example of sacrificial giving in 1 Chronicles 21:18–26?

   _____

   _____

4. In what ways should 1 Corinthians 16:2 guide how we share?

   _____

   _____

5. Describe someone who is "rich toward God." (Luke 12:21)

   _____

   _____

Personal Reflection

"Become poor" seems like a distant concept for middle-class Christians. In what ways could I model Christ's willingness to sacrifice everything for others?

4
PROVE YOUR LOVE

*"I am not commanding you, **but I want to test the sincerity of your love by comparing it with the earnestness of others."***
(2 Cor. 8:8)

*"Therefore **show these men the proof of your love** and the reason for our pride in you, so that the churches can see it." (2 Cor. 8:24)*

"I am sending the brothers in order that our boasting about you in this matter should not prove hollow, *but that you may be ready, as I said you would be. For if any Macedonians come with me and find you unprepared, we—not to say anything about you—would be ashamed of having been so confident. So I thought it necessary to urge the brothers to visit you in advance and finish the arrangements for the generous gift you had promised. Then it will be ready as a generous gift, not as one grudgingly given." (2 Cor. 9:3–5)*

*"Because of the service by which you have **proved yourselves**, others will praise God for the obedience that accompanies your*

*confession of the gospel of Christ, and for your generosity in
sharing with them and with everyone else." (2 Cor. 9:13)*

Perhaps the most difficult concept that Paul addresses in 2 Corinthians 8–9 is the issue of accountability. One year earlier Paul had approached the Corinthian church about giving to the believers in Jerusalem who were suffering from persecution and poverty. The church immediately responded with a gift and enthusiastically promised more. Paul was so pleased with their initial generosity that he shared their story everywhere he went. Many other churches were motivated to give because of the Corinthians' leadership. But the Corinthians never got around to sending their gift. This was unacceptable to Paul. He was counting on their gift, the church in Jerusalem was counting on their gift, and now the churches in Macedonia were counting on their gift. Paul writes to motivate the Corinthians. His arguments should stimulate us as well.

Sharing tests your sincerity.

Paul makes an uncomfortable comparison: "I want to test the sincerity of your love by comparing it with the earnestness of others" (2 Cor. 8:8). When Jesus dined with Simon the Pharisee, a sinful woman came and washed Jesus' feet with her tears, anointed his head with oil, and poured perfume on his feet. Simon was appalled by her expression of love. Jesus knew Simon's heart and responded with the parable of the two debtors—one who owed a little and one who owed a lot. The master called in the loans of both individuals, but neither had the ability to pay. Instead of throwing them into debtor's prison, the master forgave both of their debts. Jesus asked Simon which of these two debtors would love the master more. Simon answered correctly by choosing the one who had been forgiven the bigger debt.

Simon had been stingy with Jesus. When Jesus arrived at his house, he had not even shown Jesus the customary hospitality of offering him water to wash his feet. In contrast, the woman not only washed his feet with her tears, but she anointed them with expensive perfume. Her generosity demonstrated her deep love for Christ (see Luke 7:36–50). Our willingness to share or lack thereof reflects how much we love Jesus.

The word *sincerity* means "legitimately born" or "genuine." Paul wanted to know if the Corinthians' faith was real. Sharing is an accurate heart monitor. Later in his letter, Paul encouraged the Corinthians to check the genuineness of their faith. "Examine yourselves to see whether you are in the faith; test yourselves. Do you not realize that Christ Jesus is in you—unless, of course, you fail the test?" (2 Cor. 13:5).

> **Our willingness to share or lack thereof reflects how much we love Jesus.**

Every giving opportunity is a test—not to discover what's in your bank account, but what's in your heart.

Sharing requires actions, not just words.

Initially, the Corinthian believers were excited about helping, but a year later they still had not followed through with a gift. When their good intentions didn't translate into reality, Paul wrote to spur them into action, "Now finish the work" (2 Cor. 8:11). The Corinthians hadn't just promised Paul, they had made a commitment to the Lord, which makes their unfulfilled promises even more troubling. "But I tell you that everyone will have to give account on the day of judgment for every empty word they have spoken" (Matt. 12:36).

One mark of maturity is doing what you say you will do. In Matthew 21:28–32, Jesus shared a parable about a father who asked his two sons to work in the vineyard. The first son replied,

"I won't go!" But later he repented and went to work. The second son responded, "Sure, I'll go," but he never showed up. Jesus asked his listeners which son actually obeyed. The obvious answer was the first son, because even though he was slow to respond, he still followed through. There is a big difference between lip service and actual service. Solomon describes this type of inaction in Proverbs 25:14: "Like clouds and wind without rain is one who boasts of gifts never given."

Cornelius was a Roman centurion known for his willingness to share. "He and all his family were devout and God-fearing; he gave generously to those in need and prayed to God regularly" (Acts 10:2). People noticed his actions and knew there was something special about him. But it wasn't just people who noticed. An angel proclaimed to Cornelius, "Your prayers and gifts to the poor have come up as a memorial offering before God" (Acts 10:4).

Sharing is spurred on by accountability.

Paul wanted the Corinthian church to plan their giving so they would give willingly, not grudgingly. Biblical stewardship is not about arm-twisting, guilt-tripping, or any kind of manipulation. Giving shouldn't be a "have to," but a "want to." Each person must decide in his or her own heart what God wants them to give. That being said, Paul talked very directly about the Corinthians' responsibility to give generously. Because they had neglected to follow through with their commitment, Paul sent Titus and some of the brothers to receive their promised gift. It almost sounds like Paul turned them over to a collection agency, which feels uncomfortable.

How can we apply this to today? As believers we are to "admonish one another with all wisdom" (Col. 3:16). To admonish means "putting sense into someone's head." When you admonish someone you alert them of the serious consequences of their actions. Confronting a brother or sister about sin is perhaps one of the most difficult tasks of a Christian leader. We might be willing to lovingly confront someone about open sin in their lives, but Paul confronted the Corinthians about their slow pledge fulfillment. Some pastors and churches may be reluctant to speak about giving, but Paul instructed Timothy to be bold about encouraging generosity. "Command those who are rich in this present world...to be rich in good deeds, and to be generous and willing to share" (1 Tim. 6:17–18).

Sharing confirms that your faith is real.

Paul refers to generous giving as "the service by which you have proved yourselves" (2 Cor. 9:13). James warns about dead faith that consists of only warm, fuzzy words, but no actions. He shares a scenario of how we should respond to someone in need: "Suppose a brother or a sister is without clothes and daily food. If one of you says to them, 'Go in peace; keep warm and well fed,' but does nothing about their physical needs, what good is it? In the same way, faith by itself, if it is not accompanied by action, is dead" (James 2:15–17). Generous giving is a tangible way to move your theology from your head to your heart to your hands. Paul urged the Corinthian church to respond generously so that their faith would not "prove hollow" (2 Cor. 9:3). Good intentions aren't enough; God requires obedience.

> **"Command those who are rich in this present world... to be rich in good deeds, and to be generous and willing to share"** (1 Tim. 6:17–18).

Perhaps you've heard this thought-provoking question: "If you were on trial for being a Christian, would there be enough evidence to convict you?" Paul was looking for hard evidence of the Corinthians' faith. "Therefore show these men the proof of your love and the reason for our pride in you, so that the churches can see it" (2 Cor. 8:24). What does your giving prove about your faith?

Sue and Scott Gardner—Sharing an Obedient Gift

I was 27 years old when I heard the gospel message for the first time. That night I asked Christ into my heart. A few years later I met my husband, Scott. Together, we began to grow in our faith. Scott was recovering from a 15-year addiction to crack and cocaine, and we weren't sure if he would be able to find a job again. We both loved the Lord and wanted to obey him. In our early years of marriage we had very little, but the Lord taught us to trust him in everything, even the spiritual discipline of tithing.

Scott was making minimum wage, which was about $6 an hour. I was working full-time and making only $20,000 a year. In obedience, we began to trust God to take care of us, and he did! On many different occasions, we weren't sure if we could make a house payment or buy groceries. It was amazing to watch God work. People would show up at our door with groceries just when we needed help. We continued to trust and tithe. One time our taxes were due and we didn't have any money. I received a check in the mail that I never expected for the exact amount that I owed. God was always faithful!

Those early days of walking with the Lord were so precious to us, and we will never forget them. Scott and I spent years rebuilding our lives with the help of the Lord. We borrowed a year and a half's worth of income so I could complete my degree, hoping to find a better job, but we still remained obedient and continued to tithe.

Over the years we accumulated more things, got better jobs, and bought a bigger house. God had blessed us, but we did just as the Israelites did—we forgot him and we went our own way. When the economy tanked a few years ago, I began to stress about how we would make all of our payments. We began to justify that maybe it would be okay with God if we tithed less, or not at all. That's what we did. I put out of my mind all of those things that God had done for us and allowed the enemy to enter into my thoughts.

That was two years ago. Since then I have been anxious about our income, stressed about how to make ends meet, and even faced some difficult financial situations at work. In October, when I read a testimony of God's faithfulness to a couple who tithed through the years, conviction covered over me and I began to cry and cry. I knelt down and cried out to the Lord to forgive me for listening to all those lies the enemy was telling me. As I prayed, I sensed the Holy Spirit speak to my heart and say, "You have forsaken your first love...Repent and do the things you did at first" (see Rev. 2:4,5). I ran to Scott and told him about my conviction and together we prayed that God would forgive us both. Immediately, the Holy Spirit filled my heart with his Word and said, "Remember how the Lord your God led you all the way in the desert" (see Deut. 8:2).

Since that time, my peace has returned. The very next week we began tithing again. I know God is in control of all that we have and he knows all that we need. I think about the last few weeks and cannot believe that I allowed the enemy to steal my peace and joy in this area of my life for the last two years. God is working in Scott's job. Our finances have new priorities and, with God's help, we are working to eliminate our debt. I am trusting God to help me in my work and just this week he opened some new doors. God's faithfulness and grace are amazing.

Discussion Questions

1. In what ways does sharing test the sincerity of a Christian's love for God?

_____

_____

2. How did Cornelius prove his love for the Lord? (Acts 10:1–4)

_____

_____

3. How can Christians hold one another accountable for sharing?

_____

_____

4. Paul told Timothy to "command those who are rich" (1 Tim. 6:17–18). What role should a spiritual leader play in encouraging others to share?

_____

_____

5. How should James 2:15–17 impact our willingness to share?

_____

_____

Personal Reflection

What do my giving decisions reveal to me about my love for God?

5

SOW GENEROUSLY

*"Remember this: Whoever sows sparingly will also reap sparingly, and **whoever sows generously will also reap generously.** Each of you should give what you have decided in your heart to give, not reluctantly or under compulsion, for God loves a cheerful giver. And God is able to bless you abundantly, so that in all things at all times, having all that you need, you will abound in every good work. As it is written:*

'They have freely scattered their gifts to the poor; their righteousness endures forever.'

"Now he who supplies seed to the sower and bread for food will also supply and increase your store of seed and will enlarge the harvest of your righteousness." (2 Cor. 9:6–10)

Seeds are miraculous. Farmers and gardeners know that it requires the proper soil, water, temperature, and light conditions for seeds to germinate. In simple terms the seed has to die in order to reproduce. Jesus used seeds to picture his death and resurrection. "Very truly I tell you, unless a kernel of wheat falls to the ground and dies, it remains only a single seed. But if it dies, it produces many seeds" (John 12:24). Because of Christ's death—the one seed—"many will be made righteous" (Rom. 5:19). Jesus invites believers to follow in his steps. "Anyone who loves their life will lose it, while anyone who hates their life in this world will keep it for eter- nal life" (John 12:25). God calls

"God loves a cheerful giver" (2 Cor. 9:7).

us to work in his harvest field, but first we must die to ourselves.

The dying seed principle applies directly to sharing. The money we give becomes dead to us in the sense that we give up our control. God takes our seed and works a miracle to produce a harvest of righteousness in others. The sowing and reaping principle means that you reap in proportion to what you sow. If you sow with caution, you will reap a poor harvest. If you sow with abundance, you will reap a bumper crop. This truth should compel us to give as much as we possibly can—and then give more!

Sharing springs from a cheerful heart.

A husband who says, "It's not the gift, it's the thought that counts" is usually trying to cover for a lame gift he has given. It usually doesn't take him long to discover that the gift *does* count. However, there is a kernel of truth in this saying because our motivation for giving is what matters most. The handmade gifts children give their parents usually don't have any monetary value, but to Mom and Dad they are priceless. Our heavenly Father has a similar response toward us when we give out of love.

Giving is a personal decision. Each person should make up his or her own mind about what to share. Paul warns against two barriers: reluctance and compulsion. *Reluctance* carries the idea of sorrow or pain and describes our hesitancy to let go of our money. The saying "give until it hurts" tries to motivate us to be generous, but a reluctant giver doesn't share for fear that it will hurt. *Compulsion* describes someone's desire to pry money out of our hands. Giving under compulsion is the threat of pain from someone else. Both reluctance and compulsion thrive in an atmosphere of fear. Reluctance reveals our inner fears and compulsion exposes our external fears. God want us to be motivated by joy, not fear.

Sharing trusts in God's unlimited grace.

Prosperity gospel preachers twist the sowing and reaping principle into some sort of spiritual get-rich-quick scheme with appeals like, "Send me ten dollars and God will bless you with one hundred." Even though some misinterpret this principle, we must not minimize the fact that you can never out give God. Jesus taught, "Give, and it will be given to you. A good measure, pressed down, shaken together and running over, will be poured into your lap. For with the measure you use, it will be measured to you" (Luke 6:38).

Generous givers must overcome a major mental block that says, "What if I need my money for an emergency?" Money gives us a false sense of security. Paul warned the rich not to "put their hope in wealth, which is so uncertain, but to put their hope in God" (1 Tim. 6:17). Grace changes our outlook on money and possessions. Instead of trusting in the uncertainty of riches, we can have confidence in God's provision. The early church experienced this unlimited grace. "And God's grace was so powerfully at work in them all that there were no needy persons among them. For from time to time those who owned land or houses sold them, brought the money from the sales and put it at the apostles' feet, and it was distributed to anyone who had need" (Acts 4:33–35). Because God has no limits on his grace, we can trust him to meet our every need. God's grace releases us from our fears and frees us to give generously.

Sharing unlocks heaven's treasury.

To prove the eternal aspect of sharing, Paul quotes Psalm 112:9 in 2 Corinthians 9:9: "He has scattered abroad his gifts to the poor; his righteousness endures forever." This verse sounds like it's God's righteousness that endures forever, but it actually refers to the righteousness of the generous person. The Message reads, "He throws caution to the winds, giving to the needy in reckless abandon. His right-living, right-giving ways never run out, never wear out" (2 Cor. 9:8–11). We can give with reckless abandon because God has given us everything we have. He has even given us the ability to produce wealth (see Deut. 8:18). In a sense, our sharing is simply spiritual "re-gifting."

God lavishes his grace on us. Notice the descriptive words Paul used. "And God is able to bless you *abundantly*, so that in *all* things at *all* times, having *all* that you need, you will *abound* in *every* good work" (2 Cor. 9:8, emphasis added). The prophet Malachi challenged Israel to trust God's faithfulness. "Bring the whole tithe into the storehouse, that there may be food in my house. Test me in this," says the LORD Almighty, "and see if I will not throw open the floodgates of heaven and pour out so much blessing that there will not be room enough to store it'" (Mal. 3:10).

Sharing produces more seed.

"Don't eat your seed corn" is an old saying that financial planners use to teach investing principles. Seed can be eaten or saved and planted for next year's harvest. If you eat your seed corn, you won't have anything to put in the ground and you won't reap a harvest. In finance, "don't eat your seed corn" means "never spend your principal." When you spend something, you give up the resource itself and all that the resource could have produced in the future.

While this concept makes investing sense, it doesn't apply to God's economy. Some limit their giving to only the interest they earn and never touch their principal. Conventional wisdom tells us that if we give away the principal, we will have nothing to give in the future. Paul responds to our fear with this thought: "Now he who supplies seed to the sower and bread for food will also supply and increase your store of seed and will enlarge the harvest of your righteousness"

> **We can give with reckless abandon because God has given us everything we have.**

(2 Cor. 9:10). God promises to supply our daily bread and he also promises to meet our future needs. It's a difficult concept to grasp. The world believes that it takes money to make money, but God can make something out of nothing. God doesn't let generous sowers run out of seed. We are free to give away our seed, because he can provide more. The gifts you share to advance the gospel produce an abundant harvest of souls. It's an amazing cycle.

Gene and Elaine Getz—Sharing a Joyful Gift

I grew up in a family where no form of regular, systematic giving was modeled or taught.[12] In fact, I never considered making it a part of my Christian lifestyle until I graduated from college and married Elaine. Her family experience was just the opposite. Though her parents were small-time farmers who basically lived from hand to mouth, they still gave 10 percent of what they had and taught their children to do the same. Consequently, when I married their youngest daughter, I married a tither.

Before we were married, we decided Elaine would handle the family finances—depositing checks, paying bills, keeping records, etc. Well, you can guess what happened when I brought home my first paycheck. Elaine immediately set aside 10 percent from my gross monthly salary so we could give it to our church.

Frankly, I was concerned—even somewhat irritated. I couldn't see how we were going to make ends meet. Prior to the wedding, I had saved $750 and promptly spent it on a car—something we desperately needed. So we began our married life together with a rented apartment, a car, and a few hand towels Elaine brought, along with our wedding gifts.

But we began to tithe regularly. All of our financial decisions from that point on were made accordingly. God received our first fruits, and after that we planned our other expenditures.

In those early years as our family grew to include three children, we had virtually nothing left over at the end of each month, and the living room in our home had very little furniture (it made a great gymnasium for the kids). But there was never a day that went by that we didn't have what we needed—food on our table, clothes on our backs, and a car to drive. And when our children were old enough to receive an allowance, we showed them how to tithe. I remember laying out ten pennies and showing them how to set aside one for Jesus and his work in the world. I then took ten dimes and did the same—and then ten dollars, etc. Our children grew up understanding and practicing this concept of regular, systematic giving, and it's a part of their lives today.

I believe this is one reason God designed the tithe system. It's easy to understand in every culture of the world, and it's easy to teach our children. The facts are, if we don't model and teach giving, our kids will grow up (as most do in our materialistic culture today) giving next to nothing from their resources. In many cases, Christians have become just as materialistic as their secular counterparts.

As I reflect back on my experience as a new husband and father, I'm deeply grateful to Elaine's parents for what they taught her—and that she taught me about this important part of Christian life. Though I began tithing reluctantly, fearful we wouldn't have enough to meet our daily needs, God was never unfaithful in rewarding our obedience.

Over the years, God has honored that obedience and has enabled us to give beyond a tithe. Our goal is now proportional giving—trusting God to enable us to use any excess beyond our tithe in creative ways to help build his kingdom. To us, giving is a joyful worship experience— one that began years ago with obedience.

If all Christians gave proportionately—which God says we should— many Christians in our affluent society would be giving much more than a single tithe. There are believers in America who could easily set aside 50 percent or more of their income for God's work and still have more than enough to meet their own needs. Thankfully, some believers are this generous.

Discussion Questions

1. In what ways might people misuse the principle of sowing and reaping generously?

   _____

   _____

2. What fears cause believers to be reluctant to share?

   _____

   _____

3. What red flags indicate someone is giving out of compulsion?

   _____

   _____

4. How do you react to the promise of 2 Corinthians 9:8?

   _____

   _____

5. How should God's promise to "increase your store of seed" (2 Cor. 9:10) influence a believer's giving?

   _____

   _____

Personal Reflection

Am I truly a cheerful giver?

6

BE GENEROUS ON EVERY OCCASION

*"You will be enriched in every way **so that you can be generous on every occasion**, and through us your generosity will result in thanksgiving to God.*

"This service that you perform is not only supplying the needs of the Lord's people but is also overflowing in many expressions of thanks to God. Because of the service by which you have proved yourselves, others will praise God for the obedience that accompanies your confession of the gospel of Christ, and for your generosity in sharing with them and with everyone else. And in their prayers for you their hearts will go out to you, because of the surpassing grace God has given you. Thanks be to God for his indescribable gift!" (2 Cor. 9:11–15)

Generous giving is God's method for funding his mission. Freewill offerings support missionaries who evangelize, pastors who shepherd, Christian school teachers who train, and outreach workers who care. Without sharing, everything in the church comes to a screeching halt. The reason God pours out his abundant grace on us is to empower us to be generous in every possible way.

Perhaps you've heard the saying, "going to the well once too often." It's a phrase from the fourteenth century that means don't go to your source, or "the well," too often or it may dry up on you. When athletes train too hard they "go to the well too often" and expend all of their energy too soon, causing their performance to suffer. However, this verse teaches that generous givers will never run out of the resources to share with others.

Sharing should be a lifestyle, not a one-time gift.

"You will be enriched in every way so that you can be generous on every occasion" (2 Cor. 9:11). God is not promising to make every generous giver a millionaire, but he is saying that if your heart is generous, he will bring you opportunities to share and the ability to respond. Generous givers share every chance they get. You aren't going to the well too often. You *are* the well—and God promises to resupply you. Jesus said that those who believed in him would spring forth "rivers of living water" (John 7:38). God's grace overflows in our lives so much that we have an abundance of grace to share with others. This happens spiritually as you share God's love with others, and it happens physically when you give generously.

> **Generous givers will never run out of the resources to share with others.**

The Philippian believers demonstrated their love for Paul by their actions. When he was planting the church in Thessalonica, the Philippians sent gifts time and time again. Other churches knew about Paul's needs, but the Philippians actually stepped up and did something about them. Paul commented that they were the only church who had shared with him (see Phil. 4:16–19). Because the Philippian believers gave generously, Paul promised that God would supply all their needs "according to the riches of his glory in Christ Jesus" (Phil. 4:19). Their well never ran dry.

Sharing meets physical and spiritual needs.

Practically speaking, sharing puts your money to work. Missionaries use support to lease meeting space, purchase training materials, and fund their church plants. Bible translators purchase computers and software to speed up the tedious work of converting the Word into the heart languages of unreached people. Pastors and youth pastors receive salaries so they can focus their full-time efforts on feeding the flock. Generous giving funds people, programs, and property to advance the Gospel.

When Jesus sent the Twelve out to preach, he instructed them to take nothing with them, "no bread, no bag, no money in your belts" (Mark 6:8). They were to rely solely on the generosity of those who would listen to their message. We should give generously to support our pastors, who faithfully preach the Word. Paul told the Galatians, "The one who receives instruction in the word should share all good things with their instructor" (Gal. 6:6). Your local church should be first on your giving list, but God might be calling you to meet many other needs as well. "Therefore, as we have opportunity, let us do good to all people, especially to those who belong to the family of believers" (Gal. 6:10). Paul encourages us to be generous to as many people as we can, and he places a special emphasis on helping other believers.

Sharing brings praise to God.

Sharing and worship go hand in hand. When God answers someone who has been fervently praying for a need, their first reaction is to thank God for his provision! Philanthropists give to feel good and receive man's recognition, but stewards give so God can receive all the glory. The world views giving on a horizontal level, but Christians should view sharing as a heavenly exchange. After all, God is the one who gives us the resources to give back to him. Have you ever thought that your willingness to share causes missionaries, pastors, teachers, and Christian workers to break out in praise?

When King David asked the elders to give to build the temple, he gave generously and then he asked the elders to give. Their generosity inspired everyone else. "The people rejoiced at the willing response of their leaders, for they had given freely and wholeheartedly to the LORD" (1 Chron. 29:9). David and the people praised God for the opportunity to give. David expressed how we should feel when we give generously, "LORD our God, all this abundance that we have provided for building you a temple for your Holy Name comes from your hand, and all of it belongs to you" (1 Chron. 29:16). Everything we have is God's and we should count it a privilege to give it back to him.

Sharing prompts prayer.

On a short term mission trip to Kenya, Jim met a 13-year-old boy named Peterson who had endured an incredible amount of pain in his short life. His parents died when he was only seven years old. His uncles didn't want to be bothered, so they pushed him out to the street. For three years, Peterson lived under bridges, searched for water every day, and ate green leaves to survive. Eventually, a pastor rescued him and took him to an orphanage. Before returning home, Jim and the team gave a gift to supply the orphanage with rice for a year. He also gave Peterson his Bible and encouraged him to read it every day.

Three years later, Jim returned to Kenya. Peterson was there to greet him with these words: "I have been reading the verse you told me to read." Embarrassed, Jim asked, "What verse was that?" Peterson proudly quoted Joshua 1:8, "Keep this Book of the Law always on your lips; meditate on it day and night, so that you may be careful to do everything written in it. Then you will be prosperous and successful." Peterson added, "I get up at 3:30 a.m. every morning to study the Bible because I teach devotions to my classmates at school. Someday, I want to go to school to be a pilot, and then I want to become a real pastor." Jim was amazed how God used his comments from three years earlier to make such a lasting impact.

> **"It is more blessed to give than to receive"** (Acts 20:35).

Then Peterson shared something truly remarkable. "Every day since you left, I have been praying for you." This beautiful exchange illustrates exactly what happens when a person gives generously. "And in their prayers for you their hearts will go out to you, because of the surpassing grace God has given you" (2 Cor. 9:14).

Jesus is the ultimate example of sharing. He taught, "It is more blessed to give than to receive" (Acts 20:35). Paul could only respond with praise. "Thanks be to God for his indescribable gift!" (2 Cor. 9:15). Miraculous things happen when we act like Christ and give generously. Are you sharing with the same reckless abandon that Jesus shared with you?

Paul Johnson—Sharing a Living Gift

My first association with tithing and stewardship as well as an example of faithfulness goes back to my mom.[13] She believed that 10 percent of our family's income was to be given to the Lord's work. Every week, she would take out $1.50 and put it in a small box that she hid in the linen closet. At the end of the month she had six dollars saved up of what she called the "Lord's money." She gave three dollars to our church and sent a dollar to each of three radio preachers that she said were feeding her spiritually.

When I got my first job in the shoe store and came home with my first pay, she said to me, "Remember, 10 percent belongs to the Lord. It is not yours. It is holy money. Don't touch it!" As a result of her instruction and believing that that's what the Lord would have me do, I began to tithe my income.

My wife, Marilyn, grew up in a family that also tithed. When we got married, tithing just came naturally to us and we gave 10 percent of our income to our church and/or other ministries. About a year or so after we got married, we heard a sermon on giving. The pastor challenged us that if we really loved the Lord and were thankful for what he had done for us, we would give over and above the 10 percent as a love offering. We didn't want to get carried away with the concept, so we decided to give 11 percent the next year.

At the end of that year we had more money left over than the year before, so we decided to do it again. We pledged 12 percent for the following year. Again our income increased, and we were ahead of the year before. The Lord continued to bless us. From then on we increased our giving at least 1 percent per year and we saw our income increase. Each year we had as much or more than we had the year before. R. G. LeTourneau, who manufactured earth moving equipment, used to say, "We shovel it out, and God shovels it back, but God has a bigger shovel!" We followed that practice for fifty-five years, before Marilyn passed away.

Most people have a fixed salary that might not increase like our income did, but everyone can give 10 percent. People often ask me about my priorities in giving and how much to give and/or who to give to. How much to give is not really the question. I think we should give all we can. So the question should be, in some cases, how much to keep for ourselves? I encourage you to never miss a generous impulse. If you have a thought about being generous, respond to that thought, idea, or impulse. It did not likely come from the devil. It is a prompting of God. Therefore, give it serious consideration.

I believe that everything I have belongs to God. He owns it all. I am just a caretaker or steward of his resources.

Discussion Questions

1. Christians often quote Philippians 4:19, "And my God will meet all your needs according to the riches of his glory in Christ Jesus." How does Philippians 4:14–18 expand your understanding of this promise?

    _____

    _____

2. Think of a missionary you know. List the ways they might use their financial support to spread the Gospel.

    _____

    _____

3. In what ways has sharing impacted your worship?

    _____

    _____

4. Where do you rank your local church on your giving list? Why?

    _____

    _____

5. What criteria do you use to set your giving priorities?

    _____

    _____

Personal Reflection

In a personal moment of worship, praise God for his indescribable gift of Jesus Christ.

CONCLUSION

Generous and Willing to Share

Sharing is not easy. Deciding to share is the first step, but then comes the challenge of deciding to whom to give, when, for what purpose, how, and how much. Paul reminds us that giving is an individual decision. "Each of you should give what you have decided in your heart to give" (2 Cor. 9:7). But how can I trust my heart to guide me when my heart is "deceitful above all things?" (Jer. 17:9). Sharing is more than an intellectual decision. If we relied on our logic, we would never consider giving "beyond our ability" (see 2 Cor. 8:3).

Moses asked the children of Israel to share their resources to build the Tabernacle, "and everyone who was willing and whose heart moved them came and brought an offering to the Lord for the work on the tent of meeting" (Exod. 35:21). Sharing is a spiritual discipline. You will make the right giving decisions when you listen to the Spirit's voice.

Charlie DeLano—Sharing a Sacrificial Gift

When Charlie DeLano was seven years old, the Holy Spirit prompted him to share. Charlie has been deaf in one ear for his entire life, but that didn't prevent him from hearing God's voice.

God brought Josh Buck into Charlie's life. At the time, Josh was a 30-year-old pastor who had just experienced a tragic accident while on vacation in Cancun. Josh went for a swim and dove horizontally into a wave, but the force of the wave smashed him into the ocean floor and broke his neck. In one instant Josh was transformed from a tri-athlete into a quadriplegic.

A few months later, some churches in Grand Rapids, Michigan, banded together to build a house for Josh and his family that could accommodate his physical challenges. The Bucks visited Charlie's church and shared their testimony. That morning Charlie's pastor preached a sermon from Acts 2 about how the early church sold their possessions to help others. The next day, Charlie asked his mother, Lisa, if he could sell his bed and give the money to help Josh. He even asked if his family could sell their house, give the money, and go live with their grandparents until they found something else. Lisa told Charlie that his idea was sweet, but that he should come up with something else.

Later that week, Charlie organized an impromptu garage sale, but he only earned two dollars. So he printed up a flyer about Josh's story, went door to door, and collected 550 cans and bottles—but that still wasn't enough for Charlie.

Charlie's hearing loss now enters the story. Charlie has single-sided deafness, but the DeLanos' health insurance wouldn't cover a hearing aid. Ironically, the insurance covered hearing aids for Charlie's two-year-old brother because he is deaf in both ears. His parents, Matt and Lisa, had been budgeting for a hearing aid, and Charlie himself had saved several hundred dollars from Christmas and birthday gifts toward the $1,700 goal.

On Saturday, Charlie announced to his mom that he wanted to give the money he had saved for his hearing aid. Lisa didn't think that was a good idea, but Charlie said, "Mom, if I give with a loving heart and help others, God will bless me. I will get my hearing aid someday. They need a house now."

Toward the end of the service that Sunday, the congregation was invited to come forward with their gifts for the Bucks. When Charlie emptied the contents of his plastic baggie and returned to his seat, Lisa couldn't help but cry because she knew how much he had sacrificed.

The pastor closed the service with some stories about sharing that he had heard that week. Lisa was stunned when he started telling about Charlie. She had casually told some of her friends about Charlie's decision, but she wasn't expecting this. Charlie heard his name mentioned and thought he might be in trouble. He didn't notice the hundreds of people around him with tears in their eyes as the pastor told his story and said, "No kid ought to give away money that was intended for his hearing aid." Then the pastor surprised everyone with, "Charlie, we're going to buy your hearing aid for you!"

In the car on the way home, Lisa asked Charlie if he understood what just happened:

Charlie: "What makes me so special that everyone gave? Why would someone who doesn't even know me get me a hearing aid?"

Lisa: "Why did you want to give so badly to help the Buck family?"

Charlie: "Because if you have Jesus in your heart, you know it's the right thing to do."

Lisa: "Well, someone else has Jesus in their heart and was listening when God said he wanted you to have a hearing aid."

Charlie: "Wow! It really worked! I prayed like twenty times for a hearing aid and God heard me!"

Charlie's story sounds similar to another little boy who shared five loaves and two fish (see John 6:1–13). Jesus took it, blessed it, and multiplied it far beyond that boy's ability.

FINAL THOUGHTS FROM THE AUTHOR

The Holy Spirit has blessed some Christians with the spiritual gift of giving. "We have different gifts, according to the grace given to each of us. If your gift is prophesying, then prophesy in accordance with your faith; if it is serving, then serve; if it is teaching, then teach; if it is to encourage, then give encouragement; **if it is giving, then give generously**" (Rom. 12:6–8).

Arch Bonnema is a Texas businessman with the spiritual gift of giving. When he and Sherry got married they decided to give 35 percent of their income to the Lord's work. They shared faithfully in the good years and the not-so-good years. In 1990, Arch and Sherry attended a mission conference in Atlanta. On the way home Arch said, "You know, honey, I have to admit I've been kinda feeling lately that we ought to increase our commitment from 35 to 50 percent, and that I should also give 50 percent of my business hours to the Lord's work." Arch had hardly finished when Sherry responded, "God's been telling me that for months. I was just waiting for you to confirm it with me."

I was amazed when Arch told me his story and I asked, "How do you do that?" He replied, "When you make a decision like that, in the back of your mind you're thinking, 'Wow—God is gonna really bless us now.' But it doesn't always work that way. If you give, God doesn't always give back right away. That's where the prosperity gospel is wrong. There were times when my wife and I endured some big hardships, but we kept on giving. It wasn't that my business dropped off, but I spent less time doing it. My income dropped, but my giving increased, percentage-wise. 'No problem,' we thought. 'We'll just sell some of our stuff we don't need anyway.' To make sure that we kept our promises to missions, we gave everything we had, including cashing in our retirement, and even selling our two-year-old Cadillac."

Then Arch shared the rest of the story. "It wasn't until we had given away pretty much everything over a span of six years that, all of a sudden, everything just reversed. God started building my businesses faster than I ever could have imagined. Within two years, I had more money than I had ever had in my whole life. I never used to tell anyone what I gave, but then I read about King David's incredible gift for the temple (1 Chron. 29:1–9). The passage records exactly how much David and the elders gave, and how the people were greatly encouraged by their generosity. I realized that if I told others how much I share, I could encourage them to be generous along with me."

The minute I left Arch's house, the Spirit clearly spoke to me, "You should do the same thing." I called my wife, Cynthia, and told her everything I had just experienced. That weekend I reviewed our giving budget and wondered what it would look like if we chose a goal that stretched us. The number made me stop and think. Sharing at this level sounded good in theory, but how was it possible to **give beyond our ability**? I showed Cynthia the before-and-after scenarios, and she simply responded, "Well, God promised he would bless us."

To me, the sharing principles found in 2 Corinthians 8–9 are not just theological theories, but realities. We are an average middle-class family, but now I see just a glimpse of what it means to **become poor** so that others might be rich. Our accelerated giving has caused us to **excel in the grace of giving** by pushing us harder than I thought was possible. In a very tangible way, I am **proving my love** for the Lord—not to anyone in particular, but definitely to myself.

We believe the promise of reaping generously when you **sow generously.** God might choose to bless us financially like Arch and Sherry, but he might not. If he doesn't, we are certainly laying up treasures in heaven at a faster pace than we were before. Finally, our new attitude toward sharing has prompted us to **be generous on every occasion.** We increased our giving to our local church because that's where we receive "instruction in the word" (Gal. 6:6), but we remain open to the Spirit's prompting to share with other ministries and individuals.

"The Lord Jesus himself said: 'It is more blessed to give than to receive'" (Acts 20:35). You might wonder, "Do I have the spiritual gift of giving?" That's a great question, but let's compare the gift of giving with other spiritual gifts. You might not have the gifts of serving, evangelism, or encouragement; but we should all serve others, share the gospel, and encourage one another. Likewise, you might not have the gift of giving, but we are all called to share. "Share with the Lord's people who are in need" (Rom. 12:13).

How is God prompting you to simply share?

"So do whatever God has told you" (Gen. 31:16).

2 CORINTHIANS 8–9 (NIV)

Now that you've looked closely at Paul's principles of sharing, take a few moments to read 2 Corinthians 8-9 again and listen to what God is saying to you.

The Collection for the Lord's People

8 And now, brothers and sisters, we want you to know about the grace that God has given the Macedonian churches. [2] In the midst of a very severe trial, their overflowing joy and their extreme poverty welled up in rich generosity. [3] For I testify that they gave as much as they were able, and even beyond their ability. Entirely on their own, [4] they urgently pleaded with us for the privilege of sharing in this service to the Lord's people. [5] And they exceeded our expectations: They gave themselves first of all to the Lord, and then by the will of God also to us. [6] So we urged Titus, just as he had earlier made a beginning, to bring also to completion this act of grace on your part. [7] But since you excel in everything—in faith, in speech, in knowledge, in complete earnestness and in the love we have kindled in you—see that you also excel in this grace of giving.

[8] I am not commanding you, but I want to test the sincerity of your love by comparing it with the earnestness of others. [9] For you know the grace of our Lord Jesus Christ, that though he was rich, yet for your sake he became poor, so that you through his poverty might become rich.

[10] And here is my judgment about what is best for you in this matter. Last year you were the first not only to give but also to have the desire to

do so. [11] Now finish the work, so that your eager willingness to do it may be matched by your completion of it, according to your means. [12] For if the willingness is there, the gift is acceptable according to what one has, not according to what one does not have.

[13] Our desire is not that others might be relieved while you are hard pressed, but that there might be equality. [14] At the present time your plenty will supply what they need, so that in turn their plenty will supply what you need. The goal is equality, [15] as it is written: "The one who gathered much did not have too much, and the one who gathered little did not have too little."

Titus Sent to Receive the Collection

[16] Thanks be to God, who put into the heart of Titus the same concern I have for you. [17] For Titus not only welcomed our appeal, but he is coming to you with much enthusiasm and on his own initiative. [18] And we are sending along with him the brother who is praised by all the churches for his service to the gospel. [19] What is more, he was chosen by the churches to accompany us as we carry the offering, which we administer in order to honor the Lord himself and to show our eagerness to help. [20] We want to avoid any criticism of the way we administer this liberal gift. [21] For we are taking pains to do what is right, not only in the eyes of the Lord but also in the eyes of man.

[22] In addition, we are sending with them our brother who has often proved to us in many ways that he is zealous, and now even more so because of his great confidence in you. [23] As for Titus, he is my partner and co-worker among you; as for our brothers, they are representatives of the churches and an honor to Christ. [24] Therefore show these men the proof of your love and the reason for our pride in you, so that the churches can see it.

9 There is no need for me to write to you about this service to the Lord's people. [2] For I know your eagerness to help, and I have been boasting about it to the Macedonians, telling them that since last year you in Achaia were ready to give; and your enthusiasm has stirred most of them to action. [3] But I am sending the brothers in order that our boasting about you in this matter should not prove hollow, but that you may be ready, as I said you would be. [4] For if any Macedonians come with me and find you unprepared, we—not to say anything about you—would be ashamed of having been so confident. [5] So I thought it necessary to urge the brothers to visit you in advance and finish the arrangements for the generous gift you had promised. Then it will be ready as a generous gift, not as one grudgingly given.

Generosity Encouraged

[6] Remember this: Whoever sows sparingly will also reap sparingly, and whoever sows generously will also reap generously. [7] Each of you should give what you have decided in your heart to give, not reluctantly or under compulsion, for God loves a cheerful giver. [8] And God is able to bless you abundantly, so that in all things at all times, having all that you need, you will abound in every good work. [9] As it is written:

"They have freely scattered their gifts to the poor; their righteousness endures forever."

[10] Now he who supplies seed to the sower and bread for food will also supply and increase your store of seed and will enlarge the harvest of your righteousness. [11] You will be enriched in every way so that you can be generous on every occasion, and through us your generosity will result in thanksgiving to God.

[12] This service that you perform is not only supplying the needs of the Lord's people but is also overflowing in many expressions of thanks to God. [13] Because of the service by which you have proved yourselves, others will praise God for the obedience that accompanies your confession of the gospel of Christ, and for your generosity in sharing with them and with everyone else. [14] And in their prayers for you their hearts will go out to you, because of the surpassing grace God has given you. [15] Thanks be to God for his indescribable gift!

PRINCIPLES TO SIMPLY SHARE
From 2 Corinthians 8–9

1. **Give Beyond Your Ability (2 Cor. 8:1–4)**
   Sharing originates with God. (8:1)
   Sharing is not limited by our resources. (8:2–3)
   Sharing is a privilege. (8:4)
   Share your heart first. (8:5)

2. **Excel in the Grace of Giving (2 Cor. 8:6–7)**
   Sharing demonstrates spiritual maturity. (8:6–7)
   Sharing is best expressed in community. (8:6–7)
   Sharing demands excellence, not mediocrity. (8:6–7)
   Sharing is motivated by grace, not law. (8:6–7)

3. **Become Poor (2 Cor. 8:8, 9)**
   Sharing puts true wealth in perspective. (8:8–9)
   Sharing denies self. (8:8–9)
   Sharing is intentional. (8:8–9)
   Sharing produces eternal results. (8:8–9)

4. **Prove Your Love (2 Cor. 8:8, 24; 9:3–5, 13)**
   Sharing tests your sincerity. (8:8)

Sharing requires actions, not just words. (9:3)
Sharing is spurred on by accountability. (8:10–15)
Sharing confirms that your faith is real. (8:24)

5. **Sow Generously (2 Cor. 9:6–9)**
    Sharing springs from a cheerful heart. (9:7)
    Sharing trusts in God's unlimited grace. (9:8)
    Sharing unlocks heaven's treasury. (9:8)
    Sharing produces more seed. (9:10)

6. **Be Generous on Every Occasion (2 Cor. 9:10–15)**
    Sharing should be a lifestyle, not a one-time gift. (9:11)
    Sharing meets physical and spiritual needs. (9:12)
    Sharing brings praise to God. (9:12–13)
    Sharing prompts prayer. (9:14)

SCRIPTURE INDEX

Genesis 31:16 67

Exodus 35:21 61

Leviticus 27:30–34 24

Deuteronomy 8:2 43
Deuteronomy 8:18 48
Deuteronomy 14:22–27 24
Deuteronomy 14:28–29 24
Deuteronomy 16:16–17 24
Deuteronomy 26:12 24

Joshua 1:8 57

1 Kings 17:7–16 13

1 Chronicles 21:24 31
1 Chronicles 29:1–9 66
1 Chronicles 29:9,16 56

Psalm 50:10 30
Psalm 112:9 48
Psalm 132:1 33

Proverbs 11:25 35
Proverbs 14:23 31

Proverbs 25:14 40
Proverbs 27:17 22

Ecclesiastes 4:9–10 23

Jeremiah 17:9 61

Malachi 3:10 48

Matthew 6:20 33
Matthew 6:21 14
Matthew 12:36 39
Matthew 13:44 14
Matthew 21:28–32 39

Mark 4:18–19 15
Mark 6:8 55
Mark 12:44 29

Luke 6:38 47
Luke 7:36–50 39
Luke 9:23 30
Luke 12:20–21 30
Luke 12:21 33
Luke 19:8 22

John 1:16 12

John 6:13 25
John 7:38 54
John 12:24,25 46

Acts 4:33–35 47
Acts 10:2 40
Acts 10:4 40
Acts 20:35 ....57, 67

Romans 5:19 46
Romans 12:6–8 65
Romans 12:13 67

1 Corinthians 9:25 23
1 Corinthians 16:2 32
2 Corinthians 8:2 13
2 Corinthians 8:3 ....13, 61
2 Corinthians 8:4 14
2 Corinthians 8:8 38
2 Corinthians 8:11 39
2 Corinthians 8:24 41
2 Corinthians 9:2 23
2 Corinthians 9:3 41
2 Corinthians 9:7 61
2 Corinthians 9:8 48
2 Corinthians 9:8–11 48
2 Corinthians 9:9 48
2 Corinthians 9:10 49
2 Corinthians 9:11 54
2 Corinthians 9:13 41

2 Corinthians 9:14 57
2 Corinthians 9:15 ....12, 57
2 Corinthians 13:5 39

Galatians 6:6 ....55, 67
Galatians 6:10 55

Ephesians 2:7 ....12, 32
Ephesians 3:8 ....25, 32

Philippians 4:16–19 54
Philippians 4:19 55

Colossians 3:16 40

1 Timothy 6:9 31
1 Timothy 6:10 31
1 Timothy 6:17 47
1 Timothy 6:17–18 41
1 Timothy 6:19 14

Hebrews 10:24 23
Hebrews 11:26 33
Hebrews 13:16 9

James 2:15–17 41

Revelation 2:4 43
Revelation 21:10–21 30

NOTES

[1] www.givingpledge.org.

[2] Rose, Charlie. (2013, November 17). *The Giving Pledge: A new club for billionaires.* Retrieved February 11, 2014, from 60 Minutes: http://www.cbsnews.com/news/the-giving-pledge-a-new-club-for-billionaires/

[3] Sears, William. (n.d.). *11 Ways to Teach Your Child to Share.* Retrieved March 18, 2014 from Ask Dr. Sears: http://www.askdrsears.com/topics/parenting/discipline-behavior/morals-manners/11-ways-teach-your-child-share#

[4] O'Brien, John Maxwell. *Alexander the Great: The Invisible Enemy: A Biography* (London: Routledge, 1994), 101.

[5] Chaplin, Jane D. *Livy: Rome's Mediterranean Empire: Books 41-45 and the Periochae* (Oxford: Oxford University Press, 2007).

[6] Blomberg, Craig L. *1 Corinthians (The NIV Application Commentary)* (Grand Rapids, MI: Zondervan, 1995), 19.

[7] Barna Group. (2013, April 12). *American Donor Trends.* Retrieved March 18, 2014 from Barna Group: https://www.barna.org/barna-update/culture/606-american-donor-trends#.UyiEBmdOVMs

[8] Blackaby, Henry. (2002, March 2). *Experiencing God in Giving: Seeing Your Giving from God's Perspective.* Retrieved December 13, 2013, from Generous Giving: http://library.generousgiving.org/articles/display.asp?id=131

[9]Davis, Katie and Clark, Beth. *Kisses from Katie* (New York: Howard Books, 2011), xvii.

[10] Morris, Nathan. [NathanWMorris]. (2013, July 21). The speed of your success . Retrieved from (twitter) : https://twitter.com/NathanWMorris/status/359000405641920512

[11] Ramsey, Dave. (2009, Dec 29). Our Favorite Dave Quotes of 2009. Retrieved 2 2014, January, from daveramsey.com: http://www.daveramsey.com/article/our-favorite-dave-quotes-of-2009/lifeandmoney_other/

[12] Personal conversation. To learn more about Dr. Gene Getz's perspectives on generous giving read *Rich in Every Way: everything God says about money and possessions* (West Monroe, LA: Howard Publishing, 2004), 167–169.

[13] Personal conversation. To learn more about Paul Johnson's testimony read, My Cup Runneth Over: The Story of Paul H. Johnson (Birmingham, MI: Paul H. Johnson, Inc., 2013), 248–255.

ABOUT THE AUTHOR

Ron Haas, Vice President
The Timothy Group

 Ron has served the Lord as a pastor, the vice president for advancement of a Bible college, a Christian foundation director, a board member, and a fundraising consultant. He regularly presents fundraising workshops at ministry conferences, and has written fundraising articles for *At the Center* magazine, and Christian Leadership Alliance's *Outcomes* magazine.

Ron and his wife, Cynthia, live in Grand Rapids, Michigan, and are members at Calvary Church where Ron has served as an elder and teaches an Adult Sunday Class. Cynthia is a music teacher and an accomplished pianist. They are blessed with three adult sons.

the**TIMOTHY**group
VISION. EXPERIENCE. LEADERSHIP.

Since 1990, The Timothy Group has been helping Christian organizations apply biblical stewardship principles to their fundraising efforts. Their services include pre-campaign studies, capital campaigns, major donor programs, strategic planning, program planning studies, development assessments, executive mentoring, board training, and recruitment.

www.timothygroup.com

For information on how to purchase multiple copies of *Simply Share* for your small group, Sunday school class or congregation, please contact:

The Timothy Group
1663 Sutherland Dr. SE
Grand Rapids, MI 49508
616-224-4060
www.timothygroup.com
simplyshare@timothygroup.com